Fry It, You'll Like It!

99 Recipes to Overcome Fear of Frying

Olivia Friedman

CHAMPION PRESS, LTD.

Copyright © 2002 by Champion Press, Ltd.

All rights reserved. No part of this book may be reproduced or transmitted in any form or by any means, electronic or mechanical, including photocopying, recording, or by any information and retrieval system, without permission in writing from the copyright owner.

This book was printed in the United States of America.

For multiple sales or group discounts contact Champion Press, Ltd., 500 West Bradley Road, A129, Fox Point, WI 53217
www.championpress.com

2 | FRY IT, YOU'LL LIKE IT!

Contents

Awesome Appetizers

Basic Deep Fry Batter	11
Fried Cheese Puffs	12
Louisiana Corn Fritters with Bourbon Dipping Sauce	13
Bourbon Dipping Sauce	14
Corn Fritters	15
Spicy Chili Corn Fritters	16
Crab Fritters	17
Nutty Fried Mushrooms	18
Deep Fried Potato Wedges	19
Southern-Fried Sweet Potato Chips	20
Practically Perfect Potato Chips	21
Triple-Dipped Fried Veggies	22
Deep Fried Artichokes	23
Quesadilla Appetizers	24
Caribbean Plantains	25
Hush Puppies	26
Chinese Chicken Wings	27
Deep Fried Mediterranean Olives	28
Won Ton Shrimp	29
Deep Fried Pickled Okra	30
Easy Eggrolls	31
Deep Fried Clams	32
Deep Fried Pickles	33
Deep Fried Tuna Shells	34
Chili Cheese Balls	35
Chinese Shrimp Balls	36
Pepperoni Balls	37
Feta Cheese Poppers	38
Blossoming Onion	39
Sauerkraut Balls	40
Deep Fried Pretzels	41
Deep Fried Zucchini	42
Pasta Bow Tie Snacks	43

FRY IT, YOU'LL LIKE IT! | 3

Fried and True Entrees

Chinese Wings	47
Deep Fried Oysters	48
Country Fried Catfish	49
Deep Fried Sesame Chicken	50
Crispy Fried Shrimp	51
County Fair Corn Dogs	52
Chicken Flautas	53
Choice Chicken Fingers	54
Traditional Fried Chicken	55
Crunchy Cheese Crusted Chicken	56
Cracker Chicken	57
Chicken Fried Steak with Gravy	58
Mexican Cube Steaks	59
English Pub Fish and Chips	60
Coconut Shrimp	61
Popcorn Shrimp	62
Monte Cristo Sandwiches	63
Chicken Fried Steak, II	64
Deep Fried Beef Rolls	65
Sweet-Sour Fried Fish	66
Gourmet Catfish with a Dijon Mustard Sauce	68
Alternative Fried Chicken	69
Fried Fish Mediterranean	70
Salmon Croquettes	71
Chilequiles	72
Chilequile Tomato Sauce	73
Mexican Empanadas	74
Cornmeal Crusted Calamari on Baby Spinach	75
Very Easy Fried Chicken Strips	76
Fried Sherry Chicken	77
Fresh Fried Fish Sandwiches	78
Swiss Salmon Croquettes	79
Maryland Crab Cakes	80
Chicken Meatballs	81
Deep Fried Eggplant with Tomato and Caper Sauce	82
St Louis Deep Fried Ravioli	83
Deep Fried Pork Chops and Apples	84

Deep Fried Chicken Kiev	85
Mexican Fish Sticks	86

Desserts, Sweets and Treats

Funnel Cakes	89
Fried Pies	90
Cinnamon Donuts in a Jiffy	91
Sapodillas	92
Quick and Easy Louisiana Beignets	93
Apple Fritters	94
Spiced Sweet Potato Buttermilk Donuts	95
Honey Glazed Cinnamon Pastries	96
Warm Apple Sauce with Cinnamon Croutons	97
Potato Donut Cakes	98
Fried Cookies	99
Buttermilk Donuts	100
Raised Donuts	101
Fried Ice Cream	102
Apple Fritelle	103
Deep Fried Cheesecake	104
Fried Apple Burritos	105
Fried Oreos	106
Fried Beaver Tails	107
Old Fashioned Crullers	108
New Orleans Calas	109
Banana Fritters	110
Fruity Fritters	111
Deep Fried Watermelon	112
Fried Peaches with Raspberry Sauce	113

6 | Fry It, You'll Like It!

Fry It, You'll Like It

Fried foods have their own unique flavors and qualities. For many people, the mystery of perfectly fried foods seems too elusive to be replicated at home so they save delicious fried foods for trips to restaurants.

But no longer! Here, within these two covers are remarkably easy, uncomplicated and completely delicious fried food recipes that anyone can do at home. You've got the fryer; now it's time to use it.

Having a few cooking tips with any new appliance is helpful. Here are some smart tips for smart fryers:

- Use an oil appropriate for high cooking temperatures, like peanut oil or canola oil.
- Allow your oil to cool completely before putting the plastic lid back on the appliance.
- Store the oil in a dark cupboard. You can also refrigerate cooking oil, but it should be brought completely to room temperature before using or it will cause major spattering.
- Make sure you are frying in a safe place, away from children and pets. The cord should never hang down to the floor.
- Filter your cooking oil by using a filter especially made for the appliance, or use a fine mesh strainer. The cleaner your oil, the cleaner the taste of your food.
- Discard your oil if you notice any of these problems: rancid smell, excessive smoking when hot (normal cooking temperature), off colored oil or excessive bubbling when food is cooking.
- Follow the cooking and safety directions in the fryer manual. This manual is made just for this fryer and will have good advice.

8 | FRY IT, YOU'LL LIKE IT!

Awesome Appetizers

Appetizers are good teasers before beginning a great meal, but they are also wonderful enough to be a meal by themselves. Try a few of these easy appetizer recipes and have a fryer party at home!

Remember--start with a great batter, heat your oil thoroughly and away you go! On your mark, get set, FRY!

10 | Fry It, You'll Like It!

Basic Deep Fry Batter

3/4 cup corn starch
1/4 cup flour
1 teaspoon baking powder
1/2 teaspoon salt
1/4 teaspoon pepper
1/2 cup water (soda water works really well in this)
1 egg, slightly beaten

In a bowl stir together the first 5 ingredients. Add water and egg; stirring till smooth.

Heat oil in fryer. Dip up to 4 cups of cut up veggies, or boneless skinless chicken breasts, or fish (cut into 1/4" cubes) in this batter mixture, then place a few at a time in the hot oil. Stir batter occasionally between dunkings. Fry until golden brown, turning once only, about 2 to 3 minutes. Drain on paper towels.

*For herb batter, add 1 teaspoon dried herbs.
*For garlic batter, add 1 teaspoon garlic powder.
*For beer batter, follow basic recipe but omit water and add 1/3
  cup beer (not flat).

Fried Cheese Puffs

Makes 15

1 pound small curd cottage cheese
1-1/2 cups cornstarch
2 eggs, beaten
2 tablespoon brown sugar
1/2 teaspoon salt

Blend the cheese. Mix the cheese with the cornstarch, eggs, brown sugar and salt. Roll into balls the size of golf balls.

Heat oil in fryer. Drop cheese balls into hot oil, a few at a time, frying till golden brown. Drain on paper towels and serve.

Louisiana Corn Fritters with Bourbon Dipping Sauce

Makes 15

1 tablespoon olive oil
1/2 cup onions, chopped
1/4 cup red bell peppers, chopped
1/4 cup yellow bell peppers, chopped
2 cups sweet corn kernels, (about 4 medium ears)
2 tablespoons garlic, chopped
1/4 cup green onions, chopped
3 eggs, beaten
1-1/2 cups milk
2 teaspoons baking powder
1 cup cornmeal
2-1/4 cups flour
dash of Worcestershire Sauce
dash of Hot Sauce
Creole seasoning
Bourbon Dipping Sauce (recipe follows)

Preheat the oil for frying. Meanwhile, in a sauté pan, over medium heat, add the olive oil. When the oil is hot, add the onions, peppers, corn and garlic. Season with salt and pepper. Sauté for about 2 minutes, or until slightly wilted, then stir in 1/4 cup of the green onions. Remove and set aside to cool.

In a medium bowl, beat the eggs and milk together. Season with salt and pepper and add the cornmeal, flour and baking powder, mixing until the batter is smooth. Fold the cooled corn mixture into the batter. Season with more salt and pepper, a dash of Worcestershire Sauce and hot sauce. Set aside.

Drop the batter, a heaping tablespoon at a time, into the fryer. When the fritters pop to the surface, roll them around with a slotted spoon in the oil to brown them evenly. Fry until golden brown, about 4 minutes. Remove and drain on paper towels. Season with Creole seasoning. Serve the fritters with Bourbon Dipping Sauce.

FRY IT, YOU'LL LIKE IT! | 13

Bourbon Dipping Sauce

1/2 cup diced red onions
2 cloves garlic, minced
1/2 cup water
1/2 cup brown sugar
1/2 cup teriyaki sauce
1/4 cup soy sauce
1/3 cup white grape juice
1/2 cup bourbon
1/2 teaspoon Tabasco

In a medium saucepan, place all ingredients in the exact order listed. Mix and stir after each addition. Place on medium heat and stir until mixture reaches boiling stage. Turn the temperature down to low until mixture is barely simmering and cook until reduced by about a third.

Sauce is great with deep fried, veggies, shrimp or chicken strips.

Corn Fritters
Makes 4 dozen

4 ears fresh corn
1/2 cup all-purpose flour
1 teaspoon baking powder
1/2 teaspoon salt
1/2 teaspoon ground black pepper
3 eggs, beaten

Clean the corn and cut the kernels from the cob. Turn your knife over and using the dull edge of the knife, scrape the cob to remove more corn and as much juice as possible from the cobs, catching it in a small bowl. There should be about 1+1/2 cups corn and liquid.

Sift the dry ingredients together into a mixing bowl. Add the corn and juice, the eggs, and combine thoroughly.

Heat the oil in the fryer. Drop the batter in the hot oil by the teaspoonful and fry until golden brown on all sides, about 2 minutes. Drain on paper towels and serve immediately.

Spicy Chili Corn Fritters

Serves 4

2 eggs, separated
1 bottle beer (flat)
1 cup biscuit mix
salt and pepper
1 cup cornstarch
10 ounces frozen corn kernels, thawed
1 small onion, finely chopped
1 chili pepper, seeded and finely chopped
2 tablespoons minced fresh cilantro
1 teaspoon ground cumin
1/2 teaspoon ground red chili pepper
1 tablespoon lime juice

In a medium bowl, combine egg yolks and 1 cup of the beer. Set aside. In another bowl, mix dry ingredients and set aside. Mix corn, onion, pepper, cilantro, cumin, ground pepper, and lime juice into the dry ingredients. Add liquid and mix thoroughly. When stirring add more beer if the batter too thick to stir easily. Cover with plastic wrap and refrigerate for 1 hour.

Heat oil in the fryer, meanwhile beat the egg whites to stiff peaks. Fold gently into the fritter batter. Drop batter, by tablespoonful, into oil and fry until golden brown, turning once, about 2 minutes. Drain on paper towels.

Crab Fritters
Serves 6

1/2 green pepper, finely chopped
1 garlic clove, minced
2 tablespoons butter
2 tablespoons olive oil
1/2 cup flour
1/2 cup milk
6 ounces frozen crab meat
1 teaspoon sherry
1 teaspoon paprika
1/4 teaspoon cayenne pepper
1 egg, beaten with water
1 tablespoon water
Flour
Dry bread crumbs

In saucepan, cook green pepper, garlic, and parsley in butter and olive oil until tender. Stir in flour. Add milk, stirring constantly, until mixture thickens. Add crab, sherry, paprika, and cayenne pepper to milk mixture and chill for 2 hours.

Shape into 1-inch balls. Roll in flour, then dip in egg and water mixture, then roll into crumbs. Refrigerate until time to fry.

Heat oil in fryer. Deep fry 3 or 4 at a time, turning once, until golden brown. Drain on paper towels and serve.

Nutty Fried Mushrooms
Serves 6

2 eggs
1/2 teaspoon salt
1/8 teaspoon pepper
1/8 teaspoon nutmeg
1/3 cup ground almonds or other favorite nuts
1/2 cup fine dry bread crumbs
1 pound mushrooms, washed and dried

In small bowl, slightly beat eggs with salt, pepper and nutmeg.
In another bowl, mix together nuts and bread crumbs. Dip
mushrooms in egg mixture, then coat in nut mixture.

Heat oil in fryer. Cook until golden brown on all sides, about 5
to 6 minutes. Drain on paper towels and sprinkle with
additional salt, if desired.

Deep Fried Potato Wedges
Serves 4

1/2 cup flour
1 teaspoon garlic powder
3/4 teaspoon pepper
1/4 teaspoon celery salt
1/4 teaspoon salt
4 medium potatoes, scrubbed (do not peel)
1 egg, beaten
Bottled Ranch dressing for dipping

Mix flour and spices in shallow dish. Cut potatoes into 1/2 - inch thick wedges. Dip potato slices into the beaten egg, then into flour mixture.

Heat oil in fryer. Cook until golden brown, about 5 to 7 minutes. Drain on paper towels. Serve with dressing.

Southern-Fried Sweet Potato Chips
Serves 4

4 sweet potatoes

Salt

Peel the sweet potatoes and cut into very thin slices. Place in a large bowl, add water to cover, and refrigerate overnight. (The soaking removes the excess starch.)

The next day, heat oil in fryer. Drain the sweet potatoes and pat dry with paper towels. Working with about one-third of the sweet potato slices at a time, drop the slices into the hot oil. Fry until golden brown, about 5 to 8 minutes. Drain on paper towels. Sprinkle with salt and serve.

Practically Perfect Potato Chips
Serves 4

4 baking potatoes (1 1/2 -pounds) -- sliced paper thin
Coarse salt

Soak potato slices in 3 quarts cold water for 1 hour, changing the water every 20 minutes. Or rinse potato slices under cold running water until the water runs clear, about 15 minutes. Drain and dry potato slices on paper towels.

Heat oil in the fryer. Working in batches to avoid overcrowding, fry potato slices until golden brown, about 1 minute. Drain potato chips on paper towels, sprinkle them with salt to taste, and serve.

Triple-Dipped Fried Veggies
Serves 6

2 cups flour
1-1/2 cups beer
2 eggs
1 cup milk
salt and pepper to taste
1 carrot, cut into thick strips
1 onion, sliced into rings
6 fresh mushrooms, stems removed
1 green bell pepper, sliced in rings

In a medium bowl, mix together 11/2 cup flour and beer with a wooden spoon; let stand for at least 3 hours at room temperature.

In a small bowl, mix eggs and milk. In yet another bowl mix together 1/2 cup flour and salt and pepper.

Heat oil in fryer.

Follow the three step dipping process. First, dip each vegetable in the egg and milk mixture. Second, dip the vegetable into the flour and seasoning mixture. And third, dip the vegetable in the beer batter mixture. Place the vegetables into the oil and fry until golden brown. Drain on paper towels before serving.

Deep Fried Artichokes
Makes 2 dozen

1 (14 oz.) can artichoke hearts, drained
1 clove garlic, minced
2 tablespoons olive oil
1 (2 oz.) jar slice pimentos, drained
1/2 cup butter
1 cup water
1 cup flour
1/4 teaspoon salt
4 eggs
3 tablespoons parmesan cheese

Drain artichokes and chop.

In a medium skillet, sauté garlic in olive oil for about 1 minute; adding chopped artichokes and drained pimentos. Cook and stir until mixture is dry but not browned. In another saucepan, bring butter, water, and salt to a boil; add flour all at once. Cook and stir until mixture will form a ball that does not separate. Remove from heat and stir in eggs, one at a time, beating after each addition. Stir in artichokes and cheese. Refrigerate mixture until time to fry.

Heat oil in fryer. Drop by the rounded teaspoonful, 3 or 4 at a time into deep fryer, turning once, until golden brown. Remove and drain on paper towels.

Quesadilla Appetizers

Makes about 32

1/4 pound Mexican sausage (chorizo)
1 (15 oz.) can refried beans
1/4 cup green onions, finely chopped
1/4 cup canned diced green chilies, drained
1 cup jalapeno jack cheese, shredded
8 (7 inch) flour tortillas
1 tablespoon flour
2 tablespoons cold water

Cook sausage until done, breaking it up as it cooks. Combine sausage, beans, onion, chilies, and cheese.

Cut tortillas into quarters. Place approximately 1 teaspoon of the sausage-been mixture in center. Brush edges with mixture of flour and water. Fold in half and press to seal; keep covered as you work. Continue until all are made. Let stand 5 minutes before frying to allow edges to stick together.

Heat oil in fryer. Cook 3 or 4 at a time until golden brown, about 2 minutes. Drain on paper towels.

Caribbean Plantains

Serves 4 as an appetizer

2 green plantains, cut into 2" rounds
salt and pepper

Heat oil in fryer. When oil is hot, place plantain rounds into the oil and cook until browned, about 2 minutes. Drain on paper towels. Take a rolling pin and flatten fried plantain and cook again in the hot oil for another 2 minutes. Drain on paper towels again, then serve.

Hush Puppies
Serves 6 to 8

2 cups cornmeal
2 teaspoons baking powder
1 teaspoon salt
1 whole onion, minced
2 tablespoons bacon fat
1 egg
2/3 cup milk

In a medium bowl, mix cornmeal, baking powder, salt. Meanwhile, in a skillet, sauté onion in bacon fat until just limp; cool slightly. In another bowl, beat egg until light, stir in milk and onion and stir into dry ingredients to form a stiff batter.

Heat oil in fryer. Shape batter into 3-inch-long crescents. Fry in batches until golden brown. Drain on paper towels and serve.

Chinese Chicken Wings

Serves 6

14 chicken wings

Chinese Dipping Sauce
4 tablespoons soy sauce
2 teaspoons Chinese hot sauce
2 tablespoons honey
1 teaspoon ginger, freshly grated
1 clove garlic, minced

Heat oil in fryer. Split wings at each joint and discard tips; pat dry.

Deep fry 12 minutes until medium brown colored and completely cooked and crispy. Drain on paper towels.

Combine hot sauce and remaining ingredients. Dip wings in sauce to coat completely. Or place hot sauce, remaining ingredients and wings in airtight container and shake to coat.

Deep Fried Mediterranean Olives
Serves 8

20 large pitted green olives

2 teaspoons capers
4 anchovies, minced
2 teaspoons   pine nuts, ground
1 large clove garlic, minced
1/2 teaspoon ground cumin
1/2 teaspoon paprika
1/2 teaspoon dried thyme
1/4 teaspoon black pepper
3/4 cup flour
1-1/2 teaspoons, baking powder
1/8 teaspoon salt
1/4 cup milk
2 tablespoons olive oil
1/3 cup water
1 egg white, beaten till soft peaks form

Soak olives in 3 cups cold water for 20 minutes, changing water after 10 minutes. Drain olives and pat them dry.

Meanwhile, mix next eight ingredients in a small bowl to make the filling. Use the point of a small knife to carefully stuff each olive. Use 1/4 teaspoon filling for each olive.

For the batter, mix next 3 ingredients in a small bowl. Stir in milk, oil, and water. Carefully fold in whipped egg white.

Heat oil in fryer. Dip each stuffed olive into the batter just before placing in the hot oil. Working in batches, fry olives until golden brown, about 2 minutes. Drain olives on paper towels and serve.

Won Ton Shrimp
Serves 20

3/4 cup bay shrimp
8 ounces cream cheese
3 green onions, minced
60 won ton skins

Combine shrimp, cream cheese and onion. Place 1 teaspoon of filling in center of wonton square. Dip your finger in water and moisten two edges of wrapper. Fold and seal. Moisten one corner and fold again. Repeat until all filling is used—approximately 60 wontons.

Heat oil in the fryer and fry until golden brown, turning once. Drain on paper towels.

Deep Fried Pickled Okra

Serves 12

1 pound pickled okra, drained
2 eggs
1/2 cup milk
1 teaspoon hot pepper sauce
1/2 cup flour
1/2 cup yellow cornmeal

Beat eggs, milk, and hot red pepper sauce together until well blended. Dredge okra in flour, dip into egg mixture, and then dredge in yellow cornmeal. Put breaded okra on a baking sheet.

Heat oil in fryer. Carefully lower okra into hot oil in batches, careful not to crowd. Cook until golden brown, about 2 minutes. Drain on paper towels and serve.

Easy Eggrolls
Makes 10

3 shredded carrots
3 chopped celery stalks
1 minced onion
1 pound hamburger meat
egg roll wraps
salt and pepper to taste

Brown beef, drain well. Add carrots, celery and onion. Season with salt and pepper.

Heat oil in fryer. Lay down egg roll wrapper, fill with two tablespoons of filling and fold like a burrito. Seal edges with a little water and then deep fry until golden brown, about 7 minutes. Drain on paper towels and serve.

Deep Fried Clams
Serves 6

6 cups shucked clams
4 eggs, beaten
1 cup milk
1 cup flour
1 cup cornmeal
1 teaspoon salt
1/2 teaspoon pepper

In a bowl beat together the eggs and milk. In another bowl. Combine the flour, cornmeal and salt and pepper. Dredge the clams separately in the milk mixture and then the flour mixture.

Heat the oil in the fryer. Fry the clams for 1 minute till golden brown and take out with a slotted spoon.

Drain on paper towels. Serve with tartar sauce, seafood sauce or lemon slices.

Deep Fried Pickles

Serves 6

1 (16-oz.) jar hamburger dill pickles, sliced
1 cup whole milk
3 cups flour
salt and pepper

Spread pickles in single layer on paper towels to drain. In small bowl, pour the milk. Place flour, salt and pepper to taste in large, shallow pan. Set aside.

Heat oil in fryer.

In small batches, place pickles in milk. Then dredge in flour, separating slices if they stick together. Repeat by dunking pickles again in milk, then back into the flour. (double dipping)

Carefully drop pickles into hot oil two or three at a time (avoid crowding) and fry until golden
brown. Drain on paper towels.

Deep Fried Tuna Shells
Serves 8

16 jumbo shells, cooked and well drained (should be room temp.)
1 egg, beaten (to use in filling)
1 can tuna in water, drained
1 cup cheddar cheese, shredded
2 tablespoons green onions, sliced thin
salt and pepper to taste
1 egg, beaten (to use in batter)
1 tablespoon water
2/3 cup seasoned bread crumbs

Cocktail sauce

In a medium bowl, stir together one beaten egg, tuna, cheese, green onion, salt and pepper. Stuff the shells with the tuna mixture.

Heat oil in fryer. In a small bowl, stir together other beaten egg and water. In another small bowl, place seasoned bread crumbs. Dip each shell in the egg mixture and roll in bread crumbs. Fry a few at a time till golden brown. Drain on paper towels and serve with cocktail sauce.

Chili Cheese Balls

Makes 72

2 tablespoons chopped Jalapeno chilies
1 cup grated Parmesan cheese
1 (8 oz.) package cream cheese
2 egg yolks
1/2 cup finely chopped almonds
Seasoned bread crumbs

In a medium bowl, mix chilies, cheeses, and egg yolks together until well blended; add nuts. Form into 1-inch balls. In a shallow pan place bread crumbs. Roll cheese balls in bread crumbs; refrigerate.

Heat oil in fryer. Fry 3 or 4 at a time, until they float to the top and are golden brown, about two minutes or so. Remove from oil and drain on paper towels. Serve immediately.

Chinese Shrimp Balls

Makes about 36

3/4 pound raw shelled shrimp, minced in a food processor
1/4 cup pork fat
1/2 teaspoon salt
dash of white pepper powder
1 teaspoon sesame oil
1 egg white
1 tablespoon cornstarch

In a large bowl, mix all ingredients together until well incorporated. Cover with plastic wrap and chill for an hour or until firm.

Heat oil in fryer. Roll mixture into balls and fry in fryer. Drain on paper towels and serve.

Pepperoni Balls

Makes 2 dozen

1 loaf frozen bread dough, thawed
1/4 lb. Mozzarella cheese, cubed
1/4 to 1/2 lb. pepperoni, sliced thin

To make pepperoni balls, place 1 cheese cube on 1 slice pepperoni. Pinch off a piece of dough and shape carefully around cheese and pepperoni, to form a ball.

Heat oil in fryer. Fry in deep hot oil for about 5 minutes or until golden brown, turning once. Drain on paper towels. Serve hot.

Feta Cheese Poppers

Makes 2 dozen

24 jalapeno peppers, seeded (use plastic gloves)
1 cup tomato basil feta cheese crumbles
1 cup pancake mix

Clean out the jalapenos by cutting a slit out of the sides and carefully scraping the seeds out. Make sure you use gloves!

Heat oil in the fryer. Drop jalapenos into fryer several at a time cook for just 1 minute to soften pepper. Drain on paper towels.

In a food processor, blend feta cheese till smooth.
When jalapenos have cooled, fill with creamed feta.

In a shallow pan, pour pancake mix. In a small bowl, add a cup of water.

Dip the filled jalapenos in the pancake mix to coat. Then briefly
dip in water, and re-dip in pancake mix. Set aside until all are coated.

Heat oil in fryer. Fry a few at a time until golden brown, about 2 minutes. Drain on paper towels
and serve hot.

Blossoming Onion
Serves 2

1 large Vidalia or other sweet onion
2 tablespoons flour
1 large egg, lightly beaten
1 cup saltine cracker crumbs

Ranch salad dressing

Peel onion, leaving root end intact. Cut onion vertically into quarters, cutting to within 1/2 inch of root end. Cut each quarter
into thirds.

Place onion in boiling water 1 minute, remove and place in ice water 5 minutes. Loosen "petals" if necessary. Drain onion upside down.

Place flour in a plastic bag; add onion, shaking to coat. Dip onion in egg. Place cracker crumbs in plastic bag; add onion, tossing to coat. Chill 1 hour.

Heat oil in fryer. Fry onion 5 to 7 minutes or until golden brown. Drain on paper towels and serve with Ranch salad dressing.

Sauerkraut Balls
Makes 32

2 tablespoons shortening
1/2 cup onion, finely chopped
1 cup ham, finely chopped
1 cup corned beef, finely chopped
1 clove garlic, minced
6 tablespoons flour
1/2 teaspoon dry mustard
1 (16 ounces) can sauerkraut, drained and finely chopped
1 tablespoon parsley, finely chopped
1/2 cup beef broth
1-1/4 cups flour
1 cup milk
1 egg, beaten
1 cup seasoned bread crumbs, fine

In a skillet, melt shortening. Add onion and cook over medium heat till translucent. Add garlic and cook another minute. Now add ham and corned beef and heat through.

In a small bowl, mix 6 tablespoons flour with dry mustard and stir until well blended. Add sauerkraut, parsley, and beef broth to onion mixture, adding flour mixture a little bit at a time, cooking and stirring for 2 to 3 minutes or until mixture forms a thick paste. Spread mixture in a shallow pan; cover and chill for 2 hours.

In a medium bowl, beat 1-1/4 cups flour, milk, and egg until smooth to make a batter. Shape chilled mixture into 1-inch balls. Dip balls into batter then roll in bread crumbs.

Meanwhile, heat oil in fryer. Fry balls a batch at a time till well browned and thoroughly cooked, about 2 minutes. Drain on paper towels and serve.

Deep Fried Pretzels

Makes about 16 soft pretzels

1 cup flour
1/4 teaspoon salt
1 tablespoon shortening
6 tablespoons cold water
Coarse salt

In a medium bowl, cut shortening into flour with a pastry blender or 2 knives. Add water, 1 tablespoon at a time, mixing until dry ingredients are moistened and dough can be gathered into a ball. Knead gently a few times. Let rest 5 minutes.

Pinch dough into 1 inch balls. Roll each ball in your hands to form an 8 inch rope. Form the rope into a pretzel shape and set finished pretzels on waxed paper.

Heat oil in fryer. Fry 3 pretzels at a time until golden brown, about 3 minutes. Drain on paper towels and sprinkle with coarse salt.

Deep Fried Zucchini

Makes about 4 dozen pieces

1-1/2 cups all-purpose flour, divided
2 tablespoons cornstarch
1 teaspoon lemon pepper
1/2 teaspoon baking powder
1/2 teaspoon salt
1/4 teaspoon onion powder
1 cup milk
1 egg
1 pound fresh zucchini (about 3 medium)
Grated Parmesan cheese

In medium mixing bowl, combine 1 cup flour, cornstarch, baking powder, salt, lemon pepper, onion powder, milk and egg. Blend until smooth. Refrigerate for an hour.

Cut zucchini into 1/4-inch diagonal slices. Rinse and pat dry with paper towels. In a plastic bag, place remaining 1/2 cup flour, add zucchini circles and shake well to coat.

Heat oil in fryer. Give the batter a good stir and dip floured zucchini circles in chilled batter, allowing excess batter to drip back into the bowl.

Fry 2 or 3 at a time until golden brown, about 4 minutes, turning once or twice. Drain on paper towels. Sprinkle with parmesan cheese and serve immediately.

Pasta Bow Tie Snacks
Makes 1 pound

1 pound bow tie pasta
Seasoned salt

In a large saucepan, cook the pasta according to package directions. Drain the pasta very thoroughly, rinsing with cold water. Blot thoroughly with paper towels to access water off pasta before frying.

Heat oil in fryer. Fry pasta, a few pieces at a time, until golden brown, about 2 minutes. Drain on paper towels. Sprinkle with seasoned salt. Serve warm or cool.

44 | FRY IT, YOU'LL LIKE IT!

Fried and True Entrees

The secret to good fish and chips, or any other deep fried entrée, is how well the batter coats. The second secret is the heat of the oil.

Make sure you are generous when battering and breading your food. Don't over do it either or you will end up with dirty oil. Carefully follow each step for batter and breading, making sure to cover evenly and coat totally.

To make sure the oil is hot enough, you can test it by dropping a cube of crustless white bread into the hot oil. It should be golden brown in about

60 seconds, indicating the temperature is perfect for frying.

Lastly, make sure you use a good brand paper towel. Some are more absorbent than others.

Keep on frying!

Chinese Wings

Serves 4

8 chicken wings
4 tablespoons soy sauce
3 tablespoons oyster sauce
3 tablespoons sweet sherry
 salt and pepper to taste
1/2 cup flour
1/2 cup cornmeal

Place the chicken wings in a large glass dish or bowl. In a small bowl mix the soy sauce, oyster sauce, sherry, salt and pepper and pour mixture over chicken; turn to coat. Cover dish and refrigerate to marinate for 12 to 24 hours.

Remove chicken from marinade, discarding leftover marinade. Mix flour with cornmeal in a shallow dish or bowl and toss wings in flour mixture until well coated.

Heat oil in fryer and deep fry wings until crispy and cooked through (juices run clear) approximately 5 to 6 minutes. Drain on paper towels and serve.

Deep Fried Oysters

Serves 4

1/2 cup all-purpose flour
1 teaspoon salt
1/2 teaspoon ground black pepper
12 ounces shucked oysters, drained
2 eggs, lightly beaten
3/4 cup seasoned bread crumbs

Heat deep fryer to 375 degrees.

Combine flour, salt and black pepper. Dredge oysters in flour mixture, dip in egg and roll in bread crumbs.

Heat oil in fryer. Carefully slide oysters into hot oil and cook five at a time until golden brown, about 2 minutes per oyster. Drain on paper towels. Serve hot.

Country Fried Catfish

Serves 6

3/4 cup yellow cornmeal
1/4 cup flour
2 teaspoons salt
1 teaspoon ground red pepper
1/2 teaspoon garlic powder
6 catfish fillets
1/4 teaspoon salt

Combine the first 5 ingredients in a large shallow dish. Sprinkle fish with 1/4 teaspoon salt; dredge in cornmeal mixture, coating evenly.

Heat oil in fryer. Fry fish in batches for 5 to 6 minutes or until golden. Drain well on paper towels.

Deep Fried Sesame Chicken
Serves 4

1/2 (3 pound) whole chicken, deboned and cut into bite size
pieces
salt and pepper to taste
1 teaspoon garlic powder
1 cup rolled quick oats
1/4 cup toasted sesame seeds
1 tablespoon chicken bouillon powder
1/4 teaspoon curry powder
3/4 cup white rice flour (Asian markets carry this)
1/4 cup cake flour
1/2 teaspoon salt
3/4 cup chicken stock
1 teaspoon onion powder
1/2 teaspoon dried basil
1/2 teaspoon dried oregano

Coat chicken with black pepper, salt, and garlic powder. Chill
for 4 hours. In a medium bowl, mix together oats, sesame
seeds, 1/2 teaspoon salt, and chicken granules. Set aside.

In another bowl, combine rice flour, cake flour, 1/2 teaspoon
salt, onion powder, basil, oregano, and chicken stock. Dip the
bite size chicken into the chicken stock mixture, and roll in
sesame seed mixture. Heat oil in fryer and deep fry the chicken
till golden.

Crispy Fried Shrimp

Serves 4

4 pounds raw large shrimp—peeled, butterflied and de-veined
1 teaspoon salt
1 teaspoon ground black pepper
8 eggs, beaten
1 1/2 cups all-purpose flour
1 teaspoon baking powder

In a medium size mixing bowl combine shrimp, salt and pepper; toss to coat.

Heat oil in fryer.

In another medium size mixing bowl stir together beaten eggs, flour and baking powder. Dredge shrimp in egg mixture then fry until golden.

County Fair Corn Dogs

Makes a dozen

1/3 cup corn meal
2/3 cup flour
1 tablespoon brown sugar
1 teaspoon salt
1 beaten egg
2 tablespoons oil
1/2 cup milk
1 tablespoon mustard
1 package hot dogs
flour for dredging the hot dogs

Combine dry ingredients. Add egg, oil, milk and mustard. Mix
well to make a batter. Insert wooden skewers lengthwise into
hot dogs. Coat hot dogs with flour, then dip into batter,
coating well. Heat oil in fryer then cook for 2-3 minutes.

Chicken Flautas

Serves 4

1 1/2 cups cooked chicken
1 cup chopped onions
2 tablespoons oil
1/2 cup canned mild green chili
1/4 teaspoon ground cumin
1/2 teaspoon chili powder
1/4 teaspoon ground oregano
8 six-inch corn tortillas

Topping:
1 1/2 cups sour cream
1 1/2 cups guacamole
1 1/2 cups salsa
1 cup grated cheddar cheese

In a medium skillet, cook onions in 2 tablespoons of oil over medium heat till transparent. Add chilies, spices and chicken cooking two more minutes and set aside. Heat oil in fryer.

Carefully dip each tortilla in hot oil for a few seconds, just to soften. Then drain them on paper towels. Divide the chicken mixture between the tortillas, and roll them up, securing each one with a toothpick. Then deep fry the flautas till golden brown on all sides, drain on paper towels. Serve the flautas with a dollop each of sour cream, guacamole, and salsa. Sprinkle the top with a little grated cheese.

Choice Chicken Fingers
Serves 6

1-1/2 lb. chicken tenders, or chicken breasts cut into strips
2 cups buttermilk
2 eggs
1 tablespoon instant chicken bouillon
1-1/2 cup flour
2/3 cup parmesan cheese
2 teaspoons Cajun seasoning
2 teaspoons oregano
2 teaspoons basil
2 teaspoons garlic powder

In a medium bowl, combine milk, egg and chicken bouillon.
Place chicken strips in milk/egg mixture, and soak for 30
minutes.

In another bowl, combine flour and remaining ingredients.

Remove chicken strips from buttermilk mixture, letting as
much of the buttermilk mixture drip off as possible. Dip each
strip into the flour mixture. Place floured chicken strips on a
platter, and chill in the refrigerator for several hours.

When chicken has been chilled enough, prepare deep fryer.
Heat oil in fryer. Place chilled chicken strips a few at a time in
hot oil. Fry until golden brown and crispy. Let drain on paper
towels.

Traditional Fried Chicken

Serves 8

1 (4 pound) whole chicken, cut into 8 pieces
1 quart buttermilk
1 tablespoon salt
3 cups all-purpose flour
1 (4.7 ounce) package dry Italian-style salad dressing mix
1 teaspoon poultry seasoning
1/2 teaspoon salt
1 teaspoon ground black pepper

In a large re-sealable plastic bag, combine chicken, buttermilk and salt. Refrigerate overnight or at least 8 hours.

Heat oil in Fry Daddy to 375 degrees.

In another large re-sealable plastic bag, combine flour, Italian dressing mix, poultry seasoning, salt and pepper. Remove chicken from buttermilk, and coat well with flour mixture, tossing lightly in bag. Let set on a plate for about 10 minutes.

Fry in hot oil until meat is no longer pink, and breading is golden brown, about 20 minutes. Drain on paper towels.

Crunchy Cheese Crusted Chicken
Serves 6

1 (2 to 3 pound) cut up fryer
1-1/2 cups cheese crackers, crushed
1 teaspoon salt
1/2 teaspoon pepper
1/8 teaspoon oregano
1/2 teaspoon garlic powder
1 egg, beaten
1/4 cup milk

Place cheese crackers in a big gallon sized plastic bag. Using a rolling pin, crush crackers into crumbs. Combine crumbs with salt, pepper, oregano, and garlic powder. Place crumb mixture in shallow pan.

Roll pieces of chicken in crumbs until well coated, then dip chicken in the mixture of beaten egg and milk. Roll again in remaining crumbs until well coated.

Fry chicken in the preheated (375 degrees) oil, a few pieces at a time, removing and keeping warm till serving.

Cracker Chicken

Serves 6

30 saltine crackers
2 tablespoons all-purpose flour
2 tablespoons dry potato flakes
1 teaspoon seasoned salt
1/2 teaspoon ground black pepper
1 egg
1 tablespoon vegetable oil
6 skinless, boneless chicken breast halves

Place crackers in a large resealable plastic bag; seal bag and crush crackers until they are coarse crumbs. Add potato flakes, salt and pepper to bag and mix well. Pour into a shallow pan.

In a small bowl, beat egg. In the meantime, preheat oil to 375 degrees.

Dredge chicken pieces one at a time in egg, then place in pan with crumb mixture and turn to coat completely.

Reduce heat to 350 degrees and cook coated chicken for 15 to 20 minutes, turning frequently, until golden brown and juices run clear.

Chicken Fried Steak with Chicken Gravy

Serves 4

1 pound boneless beef top loin
2 cups shortening
1 egg, beaten
1 cup buttermilk
 salt and pepper to taste
1/2 teaspoon garlic powder
1 cup flour

1 jar prepared chicken gravy

Cut top loin crosswise into 4 (4 ounce) cutlets. Pound each cutlet thinly with a moistened mallet or the side of a cleaver.

Heat oil in fryer.

While the oil is heating, prepare cutlets.

In a medium bowl, beat together egg, buttermilk, salt and pepper. In a shallow dish, mix together garlic powder and 1cup flour. Dip cutlets in flour, turning to evenly coat both sides. Carefully dip in egg mixture, coating both sides, then in the flour again

Place cutlets into the oil, cooking until golden brown, turning once. Transfer to a plate lined with paper towels. Repeat until all cutlets are cooked.

Heat prepared chicken gravy and serve atop cutlets.

Mexican Cube Steaks

Serves 4

4 (4 ounce) cube steaks
2 eggs
3 cups dry bread crumbs
1 tablespoon dried oregano
1 teaspoon ground cumin
 salt and pepper to taste
jarred salsa on the side

In a shallow dish, combine the bread crumbs with the oregano, cumin, and salt and pepper.

In another dish, beat eggs. Dip each steak in beaten eggs, and then in the bread crumbs. Make sure to cover each steak well with bread crumbs.

Heat oil in fryer.

Place the steaks in the oil when it's hot. Cook steaks, turning once, till golden brown. Serve with salsa.

English Pub Fish and Chips
Serves 4

First the Fish:

1 pound white cod filets
2 cups flour
1 egg
1/2 cup buttermilk
1/2 cup flat beer (use a dark beer for best flavor)
1 teaspoon salt
vegetable oil
malt vinegar

Mix flour and salt in bowl, make into a well. In another bowl, mix buttermilk with egg slowly. Add egg mix to center of well and beat until well mixed. Set aside.

Heat oil in fryer. Slice the fillets into 1" by 3" strips (make sure all bones are out0. When oil is ready, add beer to batter and mix in. Dip and coat fillets with batter (it will be thick) and place into oil. Fry to a golden brown, turning once. Remove and place on paper towels.

Then the Chips,

5 medium russet potatoes, peeled

Slice peeled potatoes into ½-inch square strips. Soak in a bowl of cold water to reduce starch. Leave in water until oil is heated, then grab a handful of the wet potatoes and pat dry with paper towels until fairly dry (to reduce splattering). Place into hot oil and fry until golden brown. Fry a handful at a time, keeping cooked ones warm in the oven on a paper towel lined plate.

Sprinkle everything with salt and serve fish and chips with malt vinegar.

Coconut Shrimp

Serves 4

1 pound large fresh shrimp (cleaned, shelled, and butterflied)
2 eggs
1/4 cup water
2/3 cup corn starch
1 (7 oz.) package flaked coconut (process in a blender for best results)
1 tablespoon sugar
1 teaspoon salt
1/2 cup flour

Mix eggs and water together and set aside. Place 1/3 cup of the corn starch in bowl for dusting of shrimp.

In a separate bowl, add the remaining cornstarch, the coconut, sugar, salt, and flour, blend well. Heat oil for deep frying. Roll shrimp in cornstarch first, then in egg wash, then finally roll in coconut mixture. Place shrimp in hot oil and deep fry until done. Shrimp will float to the top when cooked. Make sure you don't overcook shrimp.

Popcorn Shrimp
Serves 4

1 pound small fresh shrimp (cleaned and deveined)
4 tablespoons cornstarch
2 eggs, beaten
1/4 cup water
1 cup saltine crackers, crushed
1 teaspoon garlic powder
1 teaspoon Cajun seasoning
1 teaspoon brown sugar
1/3 cup bread crumbs, plain
1/3 cup flour
1 teaspoon Tabasco sauce
1/2 teaspoon paprika
tartar or cocktail sauce

Place shrimp in a medium bowl and sprinkle with garlic powder, brown sugar and Tabasco. Mix well. Marinate shrimp for 1/2 hour in refrigerator.

Meanwhile, in a medium bowl, beat egg and water together, blending well, and set aside. In another bowl, mix flour, cracker crumbs, bread crumbs, paprika and Cajun seasoning together, blending well. Place cornstarch in another bowl.

Heat oil for frying. When oil is ready, take one shrimp at a time, dust with cornstarch, then lightly in egg wash, then roll it in the cracker crumb mixture. Fry until golden brown. Shrimp will float to the top when cooked—don't over cook. Drain on paper towels.

Serve with tartar sauce or cocktail sauce for dipping.

Monte Cristo Sandwiches
Serves 3

9 slices wheat or white bread
3 slices precooked turkey
3 slices ham
3 slices American cheese
3 slices Swiss cheese

Batter for sandwiches:

1 egg
1 cup water (you can add a little more water, if needed)
1/2 teaspoon salt
1 teaspoon sugar
1-1/2 cups flour
1 tablespoon baking powder
strawberry jam or cranberry sauce
powdered sugar

Place turkey and Swiss cheese on one slice of bread and ham
and American cheese on another slice of bread. Place third slice
in-between and secure the triple-decker sandwich in the
corners with tooth picks.

Place egg in mixing bowl, add water and beat together. Add
salt, sugar, flour, and baking powder. Beat batter until smooth.
Begin heating oil.

Dip sandwich in the batter and carefully cover all the sides and
surface. Carefully place batter covered sandwich in hot oil and
fry until golden brown. When sandwich has turned a warm
gold color remove from hot oil at once and place on paper
towels. Let cool for a few minutes before removing the
toothpicks. Before serving, slice into fourths and sprinkle with
powder sugar, and serve with strawberry jam or cranberry sauce
on the side.

FRY IT, YOU'LL LIKE IT! | 63

Chicken Fried Steak, II

Serves 4

8 cube steaks
2 eggs
2 cups milk, at room temperature
3 cups flour
2 teaspoons seasoned salt

In a medium bowl, whisk eggs and milk together and set aside. In another bowl, combine the flour and meat seasoning and set aside. Heat the oil.

Dip each of the first 4 cutlets in the egg wash mixture. Then dredge them in the flour, then dip them back into the egg wash, and very gently place them in the hot oil.

Cook for 3 to 5 minutes, until golden brown. Gently turn and cook another 3 minutes.

Remove from fryer and drain on a platter lined with paper towels. Keep warm. Repeat with 4 more steaks.

Deep Fried Beef Rolls

2 tablespoons oil
4 cloves garlic, minced
1-1/2 pounds ground beef
1 medium-sized onion, halved and sliced
2 tablespoons chopped celery and leaves
1 tablespoon curry powder
4 eggs
1 green onion, finely sliced
salt and white pepper to taste
1 package egg roll wrappers

In a medium skillet, sauté garlic and onion till wilted and translucent. Add celery and cook for another two minutes. Add beef and seasonings sautéing until fully cooked. Drain beef well. Mix the beef with the well beaten egg. Begin heating oil.

Place two tablespoons of beef and egg mixture on an egg roll wrapper and fold and seal according to directions on package of egg roll wrappers.

Once the beef rolls are assembled, begin frying them. Drop rolls one at a time in hot oil and fry till golden, about 3 minutes. Turn roll over and cook until that side is golden. Drain on paper towels before serving.

Serve with Chinese hot mustard or sweet and sour sauce.

Sweet-Sour Fried Fish

Serves 4

1 pound white fish, halibut, cod etc.
3/4 cup flour
1 teaspoon baking powder
1 teaspoon salt
2/3 cup water

Sauce:
1 cup pineapple juice
1/4 cup oil
1/4 cup brown sugar
2 tablespoons ketchup
2 teaspoons soy sauce
1 teaspoon pepper
1/2 teaspoon chili powder
1/2 cup rice vinegar
1 tablespoon cornstarch

Curried Fruit:
4 cups fruit (drained canned pear halves, apricot halves, peach
halves, pineapple rings, and banana slices)
1/4 cup butter
1/2 cup brown sugar
1 teaspoon curry powder

Blot halibut fillets with damp cloth and cut into 1" cubes.
Prepare batter of flour, baking powder, salt, and water. Lay fish
and batter aside and prepare the following sauce.

Sauce: In a small jar, shake the cornstarch and vinegar together
until smooth. In a saucepan, combine the other ingredients and
add the cornstarch mixture. Cook, stirring, until mixture comes
to a boil. Keep warm over a double boiler.

To cook fish: Heat deep fat in fryer. Coat halibut with batter,
and fry until golden, turning once. Drain well on absorbent
paper and keep warm. Serve the sauce over the fish

accompanied by rice. The curried fruit dish below is a gourmet accompaniment. See recipe that follows.

Curried fruit: Arrange the 4 cups of fruit in a 2 quart baking dish. Sprinkle with 1/4 cup butter, 1/2 cup brown sugar, 1 teaspoon curry powder. Bake at 350 degrees for 20 minutes, till well glazed.

Gourmet Catfish with a Dijon Mustard Sauce

Serves 4

2 tablespoons butter
1 small onion, finely chopped
1/2 cup dry white wine or vermouth
1 cup heavy cream
1/2 cup fresh parsley, finely chopped
2 tablespoons Dijon mustard
Salt or Pepper
1/2 cup white flour
1/2 cup cornmeal
2 pounds catfish, cleaned and skinned

In a saucepan, melt butter. Add onion and sauté over low heat, stirring frequently, until translucent, 3 to 4 minutes. Add wine or vermouth and cook, uncovered, over medium heat until liquid is absorbed, about 5 minutes. Add cream and reduce sauce over medium heat by 1/4, about 3 minutes.

Remove from heat and stir in parsley, season to taste with salt and pepper. Set aside.

Heat oil in fryer.

Combine flour and cornmeal. Dry fish well with paper towels, season with salt and pepper, and then dredge in the flour/cornmeal mixture. Carefully fry catfish until golden brown, about 4 minutes. Drain well on paper towels. Reheat sauce and serve with catfish.

Alternative Fried Chicken

Serves 4

3 cups canned chicken broth
4 skinless, boneless chicken breasts
5 tablespoons butter
6 tablespoons flour
3/4 cup milk
1/4 teaspoon thyme
Salt and pepper to taste
1/8 teaspoon white pepper
1 egg, beaten with 2 tablespoons water
1 cup seasoned bread crumbs

Bring chicken broth to a boil in a large saucepan. Add chicken breasts and return broth to a boil, cover, and simmer until chicken is cooked all the way through, about 10 to 12 minutes. Remove chicken and reserve 3/4 cup of the chicken stock for the béchamel sauce. Cool chicken breasts to room temperature.

Heat butter in a small saucepan. Add flour; cook over low heat, stirring constantly until flour is incorporated into the butter, about 30 seconds. While stirring, gradually add milk and reserved 3/4 cup chicken stock. Simmer, still stirring constantly, until sauce thickens, about 2 minutes. Stir in thyme and season with salt, pepper and white pepper. Cool to room temperature. Dip each chicken breast in this sauce, then refrigerate until sauce is firm on the chicken, about 1 hour.

Heat oil in fryer. Dip both sides of each chicken breast into the egg-water mixture, then dredge in breadcrumbs. Fry chicken, turning only once until golden brown, about 5 minutes. Drain chicken breasts on paper towels and serve.

Fried Fish Mediterranean
Serves 4

1/2 cup rice wine vinegar
1/2 teaspoon paprika
1/2 teaspoon dried red pepper flakes
1/2 teaspoon oregano
1/2 teaspoon ground cumin
1/2 teaspoon thyme
3 medium cloves garlic, minced
1 bay leaf
1/2 teaspoon salt
1-1/2 pounds firm fleshed fish (use tuna, swordfish, shark or mahi mahi), cut in 1" pieces
1/2 cup white flour

Mix first 9 ingredients in a medium non-reactive bowl. Add fish pieces; toss to coat. Cover and let stand at room temperature at least 1 hour. (Can be marinated up to 3 hours.)

Heat oil in fryer. Transfer fish from marinade to a sieve to drain, discard marinade. Pat fish pieces dry with paper towels, then dredge in flour.

Working in batches to avoid overcrowding, fry fish until golden brown, 2 to 3 minutes. Drain fish pieces on paper towel and serve.

Salmon Croquettes

Serves 6

2 tablespoons butter
2 medium onions, chopped fine
2 16-ounce cans canned salmon, drained and flaked
2 eggs-beaten
1-1/3 cups cracker crumbs, finely ground
salt and pepper to taste

Heat butter in a medium skillet, add onions and sauté until softened, about 4 minutes. Transfer onions to a large bowl; cool slightly. Stir in salmon, eggs, 2/3 cup cracker meal, and 1/2 teaspoon pepper. Form salmon mixture into 12 round patties, 2 1/2 inches in diameter; dredge each patty in remaining 2/3 cup cracker crumbs.

Meanwhile, heat oil in fryer. Working in batches to avoid overcrowding, fry salmon patties, turning once, until golden brown, about 5 minutes. Drain on paper towels and serve.

Chilequiles

Serves 8

1-1/2 cups Chilequile tomato sauce (see recipe)
1/2 small onion, minced
1/4 red bell pepper, finely chopped
1-1/2 cups Mexican cheese or farmer's cheese
salt and pepper to taste
10 flour tortillas
3 eggs
1/4 teaspoon salt
1 teaspoon flour
1/4 cup oil

To make filling, combine onion and the red pepper in a medium bowl. Add the cheese (1-1/2 cups), salt and pepper, and 1/4 teaspoon pepper. Spoon 2 teaspoons of the cheese mixture onto the bottom center of each tortilla, and fold tortillas in half to form a semicircle. (Don't worry about cracks in the tortillas. The egg batter will seal it. You can wrap and refrigerate filled tortillas overnight, if you want.)

Separate eggs and whip egg whites with 1/4 teaspoon salt to firm peaks. Lightly beat the yolks and flour and fold mixture into the whites. Heat oil in fryer. Dip the tortillas into the egg batter and shake off excess. Fry tortillas until golden brown, about 1-1/2 minutes on each side. Put tortillas in a single layer into two 9- by 13-inch baking dishes and garnish with Chilequile tomato sauce. Bake until tortillas are heated through, about 20 minutes.

Chilequile Tomato Sauce

3 large tomatoes, cored and chopped
1 medium clove garlic, minced
1/2 small onion, chopped
1/4 teaspoon salt
1/2 teaspoon dried red pepper flakes
1/4 cup water.

Place all ingredients in a medium saucepan.

Bring to a boil over medium heat, reduce heat to low, and simmer, uncovered, until vegetables are cooked all the way through, about 10 minutes. Transfer contents of saucepan to a blender and purée. Return sauce to the saucepan and simmer until slightly thickened, about 10 minutes.

Mexican Empanadas

Serves 4

8 Flour Tortillas

3 tablespoons sun-dried tomatoes
3 tablespoons cilantro, chopped
3/4 pound cream cheese - softened
1 cup chopped cooked chicken
Salt
Fresh ground black pepper
Cayenne pepper
1 egg
1 small hot pepper (any kind)
Salt
Fresh ground pepper

In a large bowl, mix together tomatoes, cilantro, chicken and cheese. Season to taste with salt, black pepper, and cayenne pepper. Set aside.

Lightly beat egg for sealing tortillas. Put a tablespoon of the filling in the center of each tortilla. Brush edges with egg, fold in half, using a toothpick to secure.

Heat oil in the fryer. Fry the empanadas, a few at a time, in the oil until golden brown, turning once, about 2 minutes on each side. Drain on paper towels.

Serve empanadas with salsa, sour cream and guacamole if you like.

Cornmeal Crusted Calamari on Baby Spinach

Serves 4

1/2 cup flour
1/2 cup yellow cornmeal
1/2 teaspoon cayenne pepper powder
1 teaspoon salt
1/2 teaspoon fresh ground black pepper
1 teaspoon lemon juice
1 bag baby spinach, lightly steamed
1 pound cleaned calamari (ask your fish monger to clean it)
2 lemons, cut into wedges

In a bowl, mix the flour, cornmeal, cayenne pepper, 1 teaspoon salt, and 1/2 teaspoon black pepper in a shallow dish. Put the milk into a shallow bowl and squeeze in 1 teaspoon lemon juice.

Rinse and pat calamari dry. Slice the bodies into 1/4-inch rings (tentacles can be fried whole). Heat oil in fryer. Working in batches, dip the calamari into the milk mixture, dredge in the cornmeal mixture, and deep fry until golden brown, about 30 seconds, being careful not to crowd calamari. Drain each batch on paper towels and serve on a bed of steamed baby spinach, garnished with lemon wedges.

Very Easy Fried Chicken Strips

Serves 4

4 boneless, skinless chicken breasts
1 (12 ounce) can evaporated milk
2 cups corn flake cereal, crushed
salt and pepper, to taste

Slice chicken lengthwise to make approximately 3 strips for each breast. Place strips in a large bowl and cover with evaporated milk. Heat oil in fryer.

Pour corn flake crumbs on a plate, shake excess milk off chicken strips; dredge in cereal crumbs, gently place in hot oil. Cook chicken until golden brown on both sides, turning only once. Drain on paper towels. Salt and pepper to taste.

Fried Sherry Chicken

Serves 6

1 frying chicken (about 3 pounds), cut into pieces (or if you just like white meat, breasts only)
2 tablespoons dry sherry
1/2 cup flour
1 teaspoon garlic powder
1 teaspoon salt
1/2 teaspoon paprika
1/4 teaspoon pepper,
1/8 teaspoon sage
1/4 teaspoon thyme leaves
1/4 teaspoon dried basil

Place chicken pieces in a shallow pan and sprinkle with the sherry and allow to stand for 10 minutes. In a plastic bag, combine flour, garlic powder, salt, paprika, pepper, sage, thyme and basil.

Heat oil in fryer. Place chicken, one piece at a time into bag and shake to coat. Put all pieces of coated chicken on a plate. Fry chicken without crowding one or two pieces at a time for 7 minutes each side, turning only once. Chicken should be a nice golden brown color. Drain on paper towels and transfer to heat resistant serving platter to keep warm in a low oven while you finish frying the chicken.

FRY IT, YOU'LL LIKE IT! | 77

Fresh Fried Fish Sandwiches

Makes 6 sandwiches

3 pounds firm fresh fish fillets (like cod, whitefish)
1/2 teaspoon lemon pepper
1/2 teaspoon garlic powder
1 cup pancake mix
1 cup Italian bread crumbs
1/4 cup water
1 egg, beaten
6 hamburger buns
tartar sauce

Heat oil in fryer.

Cut fish into sandwich-sized pieces. Lightly sprinkle with lemon pepper and garlic salt.

Combine pancake mix and bread crumbs in a plastic bag. In a small bowl, beat together egg and water. Dip fish in water and egg mixture and gently shake fish in bag to coat with crumbs. Fry
in oil for 7 minutes, or until golden brown, turning only once. Drain on paper towels. Place on hamburger buns with tartar sauce and serve immediately.

Swiss Salmon Croquettes
Serves 4

1 (16 ounce) can salmon, drained
1 cup milk
4 tablespoons flour
4 tablespoons butter
4 tablespoons fresh parsley, chopped
1 green onion, minced
1/4 teaspoon dried dill
1 egg, lightly beaten
2 ounces Swiss cheese,
1 cup seasoned bread crumbs
1 cup flour

Add milk to salmon liquid to make 1 cup. In a medium skillet, melt butter, whisking in flour and cook until bubbling. Gradually, stir in milk/salmon liquid and cook until thick. Remove from heat.

Add mashed salmon, parsley, scallion and dill. Season with salt and pepper. Let cool and refrigerate until firm.

Divide salmon into 8 equal parts. Cut cheese into 8 equal sticks. Wrap each stick of cheese in a salmon part shaping into a fat cigar shape. Roll each croquette in flour, then beaten egg, and finally in bread crumbs. Heat oil in fryer and fry until golden on each side, turning only once. Drain on paper towels.

Maryland Crab Cakes

Makes 8 crabcakes

2 pounds lump blue crab meat
1/2 cup butter
1/2 cup finely chopped onion
1/4 cup finely chopped celery
1/4 cup finely chopped red bell pepper
1/2 cup seasoned bread crumbs
2 eggs
1 tablespoon Worcestershire sauce
3 tablespoons mayonnaise
1 tablespoon dry mustard
1 tablespoon Old Bay seasoning
Tartar sauce
Lemon wedges

Carefully pick over all the crab meat to remove all bits of shell and cartilage. Set aside.

Sauté the onion, celery and bell pepper in butter until soft, but not browned. Mix the cooked vegetables with the eggs, Worcester-shire, dry mustard, mayonnaise, and Old Bay seasoning until well combined. Stir in bread crumbs. Carefully fold in crab meat. Form into patties, cover, and refrigerate for at least one hour before cooking.

Heat oil in fryer. Lower one crab cake at a time into fryer and cook for 2-3 minutes on either side until golden brown, turning once only. Drain on paper towels. Serve immediately with tartar sauce and lemon wedges.

Chicken Meatballs

Makes 2 dozen

1/2 large onion, chopped
1 pound chicken, chopped finely
1 tablespoon sugar
1-1/2 tablespoon sweet rice wine
2 tablespoons soy sauce
1 egg
2 tablespoons oil
3-1/2 tablespoons water
1-1/2 tablespoons sherry

In a medium bowl, combine chicken and onion with sugar, rice wine, 1 tablespoon of the soy sauce, and egg and mix thoroughly. Roll into bite-sized balls.

Heat oil in fryer. Deep fry meatballs, 2 or 3 at a time until well browned. Drain on paper towels.

In a medium pan, combine water, sherry and remaining 1 tablespoon soy sauce and cook until reduced nearly in half. Serve on the side with meatballs.

Deep Fried Eggplant with Tomato and Caper Sauce

Serves 4

1 eggplant, peeled and sliced into 1/2" slices
2 cloves garlic, pressed
salt and pepper
1/2 cup flour
2 eggs, lightly beaten
1/2 cup bread crumbs
6 tablespoons parmesan, grated
2 teaspoons sage
1 (28 oz.) canned tomatoes, drained
1 tablespoon capers
1 teaspoon olive oil

Heat oil in fryer.

Mix together salt and garlic. Rub eggplant slices well with garlic and salt, then discard mixture.

Place flour in a shallow pan and season with salt and pepper. Dredge the eggplant with flour. Dip each slice in the eggs. Mix together the bread crumbs, the parmesan cheese and sage. Coat the eggplant slices with the bread crumb mixture.

Drop eggplant slices into fryer, two at a time, but avoid crowding. Cook for 3 minutes, or until eggplant is golden brown outside, soft inside. Drain on paper towels.

To make sauce, place tomatoes in a blender, along with the capers and puree. Pour into pan, whisk in the olive oil, and season with salt and pepper and warm over medium heat till just warmed.

Serve eggplant with sauce and a generous grating of parmesan cheese on the top.

St. Louis Deep Fried Ravioli

Serves 4

1 pound frozen ravioli, thawed (filling of your choice)
2 tablespoons milk
1 egg
1 cup seasoned bread crumbs, finely ground
1 cup spaghetti sauce
Fresh grated Parmesan cheese

In a medium bowl, beat together the milk and egg. In a shallow pan, pour the seasoned crumbs. Dip each ravioli in milk/egg and dredge in crumbs.

Heat oil in fryer. Fry a few ravioli at a time for about a minute on each side till golden in color. Drain on paper towels. Keep warm in low oven till all have been fried.

When ready to serve, top with spaghetti sauce and sprinkle with Parmesan cheese.

Deep Fried Pork Chops and Apples

Serves 6

6 boneless loin pork chops, 1/2 inch thick
1 large apple, peeled, cored and sliced
2 eggs, beaten
2 tablespoons milk
1 cup dry bread crumbs
1 teaspoon ground ginger
3/4 teaspoon salt
1/4 teaspoon allspice

Pound each chop to 1/4 inch thickness with meat mallet.

In a pie plate, combine eggs and milk, mixing well. Pour bread crumbs, salt and seasonings into a shallow pan.

Dip pork and apple rings in egg mixture, then dredge well in bread crumb mixture.

Heat oil in fryer. Fry pork and apple rings, a few at a time, avoid crowding. Fry 2 or 3 minutes or until deep golden brown, turning once. Drain on paper towels and serve immediately.

Deep Fried Chicken Kiev

Serves 8

8 skinless, boneless chicken breasts
1 teaspoon salt
1/3 cup margarine
1 tablespoon minced parsley
1 teaspoon lemon juice
1 clove garlic, minced
1/3 cup all-purpose flour
1-1/2 cups seasoned bread crumbs
2 eggs, lightly beaten

Sprinkle chicken breasts with salt.

In a medium bowl, cream butter, parsley, lemon juice, and garlic together well. Spread 2 teaspoons along the center length of each chicken breast half. Roll up ends and long sides around flavored butter; skewer with a toothpick to close.

In a shallow dishes, place flour. In another shallow dish, place the bread crumbs. In a shallow bowl, place the beaten eggs. Begin dipping each prepared chicken breast first in flour, then eggs, and then crumbs. Place seam-side-down on a plate and refrigerate for at least 2 hours or until crumbs are set.

Heat oil in fryer. Cook chicken rolls in hot oil, one roll at a time until well browned, about 5 minutes or so. Remove with slotted spoon. Drain on paper towels and serve immediately.

Mexican Fish Sticks
Serves 4

1 package (9 ounces) frozen fish sticks
1/4 cup salsa
1/2 cup shredded jack cheese

Heat oil in fryer. Fry frozen fish sticks, a batch a time until golden brown, about 3 minutes. Drain on paper towels.

Preheat broiler on oven. Arrange fried fish sticks in an 8-inch square baking dish. Top with cheese and broil 4 inches from heat for 1 to 2 minutes or until cheese is melted. Serve with salsa on the side.

Desserts, Sweets and Treats

The fryer is the perfect place to make a delectable sweet or treat. Cakes, donuts and pies all benefit from the fryer treatment creating crunchy outer portions and tender middles.

Make sure your dough or battered food isn't too cold before coming in contact with the hot oil—it could cause splattering.

88 | FRY IT, YOU'LL LIKE IT!

Funnel Cakes

Makes 2 dozen

1 1/4 cup flour
2 tablespoons sugar
1 teaspoon baking powder
1/4 teaspoon salt
1 egg, beaten
2/3 cup milk

Powdered sugar

In a medium bowl, mix the flour, sugar, baking powder, and salt. Make a well in the middle of the dry ingredients and add beaten egg and milk, beating until batter is smooth.

Heat oil in fryer.

Hold your finger over bottom of a funnel having a 3/8 to 1/2 inch hole to plug it and with the other hand spoon funnel full with batter. Hold funnel as near to the surface of the fryer as safely possible; remove your finger and drop batter into hot fat, using a circular movement from center outward to form a spiral cake about 3 inches in diameter. Immediately replace finger on bottom of funnel; then form other cakes (as many as will float uncrowded).

Fry until cakes are puffy and golden brown, turning once. Lift from oil with a slotted spoon, and allow to drain for a few seconds before removing to paper towels to finish draining.

Sift powdered sugar lightly over cakes and serve warm.

Fried Pies

Makes 9 pies

4 cups flour
2 teaspoons salt
1 cup shortening
1 cup milk
8 ounces dried apricots
6 ounces dried peaches
3/4 cup white sugar

In a large bowl, mix together flour and salt to make crust. Cut in shortening until mixture is crumbly resembling cornmeal. Mix in milk and stir until dough forms a ball. Refrigerate dough for an hour.

Roll out dough and cut into 18 6-inch circles and set aside.

In the meantime, make filling by taking a large saucepan, and combining apricots, peaches, and sugar. Add just enough water to cover fruit. Cover pan and cook over low heat until fruit is falling apart. Remove lid and continue to cook until water is evaporated.

Heat oil in fryer. Spoon equal amounts of filling into each pastry circle and fold in half. Seal pastry with a fork dipped in cold water.

Fry a few pies at a time in hot oil till golden brown, turning once. Drain pies on paper towels. Serve when slightly cooled.

Cinnamon Donuts in a Jiffy
Makes 10

1 can refrigerator buttermilk biscuits (not the flaky kind)
Cinnamon sugar

Cut donut holes out by using a 1 inch biscuit cutter.

Heat oil in fryer. Fry 2 to 3 donuts at a time till brown, turning
once. Fry donut "holes" separately. Drain on paper towels.
Immediately roll just fried donuts in cinnamon sugar and serve.

Sopapillas

Makes 12

A traditional Spanish dessert made easy.

1 cup flour
1 teaspoon baking powder
1/4 teaspoon salt
4 tablespoons shortening
4 to 5 tablespoons warm water
melted butter
cinnamon sugar

Combine flour, baking powder, and salt in a mixing bowl; cut in shortening with two knives, making almost a cornmeal texture. Stir in warm water. Place dough on a lightly floured surface and hand knead until smooth. Cover and let stand for 15 minutes.

Form dough into 1 inch balls then cover. Roll each ball into a thin 3-inch circle. Cover circles with waxed paper, separating circles and stack. Pinch and pull circle edges (lightly) as you drop into preheated oil in deep fryer. Fry 1 or 2 at a time. Fry 1 minute; turn and fry 1 minute or until golden brown. Drizzle the top with butter and sprinkle with cinnamon sugar.

Quick and Easy Louisiana Beignets

Makes 2 dozen

1 package (16 ounces) hot roll mix
1/4 sugar
1 teaspoon vanilla
powdered sugar for rolling

Prepare roll mix according to package directions, but add 1/4 cup sugar to flour mixture and vanilla to the hot water. When kneading is completed, lightly "grease" the dough, using a little oil in a bowl then roll the ball of dough in the bowl to coat with oil. Cover with plastic wrap and a towel. Refrigerate for several hours or overnight.

Remove dough from refrigerator; punch down and cut in half. On a lightly floured surface, roll each half to make a 9 x 12-inch rectangle. Cut each into 12 (3-inch) squares. Cover with a towel and let rise for 30 minutes.

Heat oil in fryer. Deep fry beignets no more than two at a time. Fry until golden brown, turning once, about 1 minute or so, each side. Sprinkle generously with powdered sugar.

Apple Fritters
Serves 6

2 green apples, peeled, cored and sliced into 1/4" rings
1/2 tablespoon brandy
2 teaspoons lemon juice
1 egg
1 tablespoon granulated sugar
1/2 teaspoon grated lemon zest
1/2 tablespoon brandy
1/4 cup buttermilk (at room temperature)
1/2 tablespoon butter, melted and cooled
1/2 cup white flour
1/4 teaspoon baking soda
1/4 teaspoon salt
Powdered sugar -- for dusting

In a large bowl, toss apples with brandy and lemon juice. Let
stand 1 hour at room temperature.

For the batter, whisk egg, sugar, and lemon zest in a small
mixing bowl until it light in color. Beat in brandy, then add
buttermilk and butter.

Sift flour with baking soda and salt. Fold into buttermilk
mixture until smooth. If batter is too thick, add 1 to 2 more
teaspoons buttermilk or a little water.

Heat oil in fryer.

Drain apple slices and pat dry. Dip slices, one at a time, into
batter to coat completely. Let excess batter drip back into the
bowl. Lower apple slices into the hot oil and fry until bottom
of each slice is deep golden brown and coating is puffed, 2 to 3
minutes. Carefully turn slices and fry until golden brown on the
other side. Drain on paper towels, dust with powdered sugar
and serve.

Spiced Sweet Potato Buttermilk Donuts

Serves 4

3 eggs
3/4 cup brown sugar
2 tablespoons oil
2 tablespoons buttermilk
2 teaspoons cream sherry
1 teaspoon cinnamon
1/2 teaspoon nutmeg
1 cup mashed cooked sweet potato
3 cups flour
1/2 teaspoon salt
3 teaspoons baking soda
3 teaspoons baking powder
1 teaspoon vanilla
1 teaspoon grated orange rind

Mix all ingredients together well. This dough is very sticky, but don't add too much extra flour or they'll get too heavy.

Heat oil in fryer. Using a 2" biscuit cutter, cut out rounds. Using a 1" biscuit cutter, cut the "holes" out of the donuts. Fry donuts and holes in fryer (don't crowd) till golden brown, turning once. Drain on paper towels, serve at once.

Honey Glazed Cinnamon Pastries
Serves 10

1/2 cup vegetable oil
2 teaspoons lemon zest
2 teaspoons ground cinnamon
1/2 cup white grape juice
2 cups flour
1 cup honey
3 tablespoons powdered sugar
1/4 teaspoon ground cinnamon

Mix cinnamon, lemon zest, oil, white grape juice, and flour together in a medium bowl. Knead the dough in the bowl until smooth, about 2 minutes. Flatten the dough into a disk, wrap it in plastic wrap, and let it rest 30 minutes.

Then, on a lightly floured work surface, roll the dough into a large rectangle, about 1/8-inch thick. Cut this dough rectangle into 2- by 1-inch strips—you should get about 60 strips. Cover the dough strips with a kitchen towel and let them rest again for 30 minutes.

Meanwhile, bring the honey and 1/4 cup water to boil in a small saucepan and simmer for 15 minutes. Cover and keep warm. Mix powdered sugar and cinnamon in a small bowl, set aside.

Next, heat the oil in the fryer. Working in batches, fry the dough strips until they are golden brown, 2 to 3 minutes, turning once. Drain on paper towels.

Dip each pastry in the honey mixture, and allow to sit on a wire rack so excess honey will drain. Cool to and dust pastries with cinnamon sugar.

Warmed Apple Sauce with Cinnamon Croutons

Serves 6

3 tablespoons sugar
3/4 teaspoon ground cinnamon
1 French baguette, sliced into 12 slices
1/2 cup apple butter
3 cups warmed chunky apple sauce

Combine sugar and cinnamon in a shallow dish; stir well, and set aside.

Heat oil in fryer. Brush both sides of bread slices with apple butter and fry till golden, turning once. Drain on paper towels and top with cinnamon sugar mixture. Serve 2 cinnamon croutons with bowls of warmed apple sauce.

Potato Donut Cakes

Make 3 dozen

1/2 cup mashed potatoes (mashed with milk and butter)
1/4 cup sugar
1 egg, beaten
1/2 cup sour cream
1/2 teaspoon vanilla
1-1/2 cups flour
1/2 teaspoon baking soda
1/4 teaspoon baking powder
Additional sugar or powdered sugar for rolling

In a bowl, combine dry ingredients; stir in potato mixture, mix well then add remaining egg, sour cream and vanilla.

Heat oil in fryer. Drop dough by teaspoonfuls, 2 to 3 at a time into hot oil, but do not crowd. Fry for 1 minute per side or till golden brown. Drain on paper towels. Roll in sugar. Serve at once.

Fried Cookies
Makes 6 dozen

6 egg yolks
6 tablespoons sour cream
1 teaspoon vanilla
1 teaspoon grated lemon zest
1 Dash salt
1-1/4 cups flour
2 tablespoons flour
sugar for sprinkling

In a medium bowl, beat egg yolks, sour cream, vanilla, lemon zest, and salt together until well mixed. Add 1-1/4 cups flour, stirring to form a soft dough.

Sprinkle 1 tablespoon flour on counter top. Turn dough out onto floured surface. Sprinkle remaining flour over surface. Pat and roll dough to form a 16 inch square. Let stand a few minutes before cutting. Make 8 cuts (2-inches apart) across one side and 5 cuts across the other side. You should have 42 rectangles. Cut these each diagonally to make 84 triangles.

Heat oil in fryer. Cook 3 or 4 at a time, turning once until golden brown (about 2 minutes). Drain on paper towels. Sprinkle with sugar.

Buttermilk Donuts

Makes 2 1/2 dozen

2 eggs beaten
1 cup sugar
1 cup buttermilk
2 tablespoons melted shortening
3-1/2 cups flour
1 teaspoon baking powder
1 teaspoon baking soda
1 teaspoon salt
1/2 teaspoon nutmeg

In a large bowl, beat eggs and sugar together. Add in the buttermilk and melted shortening. In another bowl, sift flour with baking powder, baking soda, salt and nutmeg. Stir into the egg mixture and mix well.

Heat oil in fryer. Turn out dough onto a floured board, kneading lightly, then roll out and cut. Fry one at a time till golden, turning once. Drain on paper towels and serve at once.

Raised Donuts
Makes 45

Start these luscious donuts the night before you plan to make them.

1 cup sugar
1 cup milk, scalded
2 tablespoons melted margarine
1/2 teaspoon salt
2 eggs, well beaten
2 cups flour (approximately)
1 envelope dry yeast
1/4 cup lukewarm water
1/4 teaspoon cinnamon

The night before, scald milk and add butter and salt. Allow yeast to soften in warm water while mixture is cooling. When mixture is lukewarm, add yeasty water. Add enough flour to make a soft dough. Cover and let rise overnight.

Next morning, punch down dough, add sugar, eggs, and enough additional flour to form a soft dough. Cover and let rise until doubled. Turn dough onto lightly floured board roll into one big sheet 1/3-inch thick, cut with lightly floured donut cutter.

Heat oil in fryer. Cook in fryer one at a time till golden, turning once. Drain on paper towels. Serve.

FRY IT, YOU'LL LIKE IT! | 101

Fried Ice Cream
Serves 8

1 quart vanilla ice cream
3 cups crushed cornflakes cereal
1 teaspoon ground cinnamon
3 egg whites

Scoop ice cream into 8 - 1/2 cup sized balls. Place on baking sheet and freeze until firm, about 1 hour.

In a shallow dish, combine cornflakes and cinnamon. In a medium bowl, beat egg whites until foamy. Roll ice cream balls in egg whites, then in cornflake mixture, covering ice cream completely. Repeat if necessary. Freeze again until firm, at least 3 hours.

Heat oil in fryer. Fry ice cream balls 1 or 2 at a time, for 10 to 15 seconds, until golden brown. Remove with slotted spoon and drain on paper towels for a few seconds and serve immediately.

Apple Fritelle

Serves 6

2 pounds apples, peeled, cored and shredded
4 large eggs
2 cups flour
4 tablespoons sugar
2 teaspoons rum
4 tablespoons milk
grated zest from two lemons
powdered sugar

In a bowl, beat eggs, add the sugar and the flour. Mix until well-combined then add rum, milk and the grated lemon zest. Add the apples and mix until well incorporated.

Heat the oil in the fryer. Shape into balls and drop in hot oil and cook till golden on all sides. Drain on paper towels and sprinkle with powdered sugar and serve immediately.

Deep Fried Cheesecake

Makes 30 pieces

1 prepared cheesecake (homemade or bought)
30 egg roll wrappers (available in the produce department)
1 egg, beaten
1 cup milk

Cinnamon sugar

In a small bowl, mix together egg and milk. Cut already-baked cheesecake into pieces approximately 3 x 1-inches in size. One large cheesecake will produce about 30 slices for deep frying.

Lightly moisten each spring roll wrapper with the egg mixture. Blot off excess egg mixture with a paper towel.

Place each piece of cheesecake in the middle of a wrapper. Fold top of wrapper down over the cheesecake, and both sides toward the middle. Roll each piece of cheesecake toward you until it is completely rolled up. Check to make sure the dough is sealed completely.

Heat oil in fryer. When the oil is ready, cook cheesecakes one at a time in the oil and allow to brown lightly, approximately 10 seconds. Drain deep-fried slices of cheesecake on paper towels and sprinkle with cinnamon sugar.

Fried Apple Burritos

Serves 6

6 medium (7 inch) flour tortillas
1 (20 oz.) can apple pie filling

Powdered sugar

Warm tortillas in microwave oven for 10 seconds for easy
rolling. Place about 2 tablespoons apple filling near center of
each tortilla. Fold back flap over filling, fold in sides and secure
with a toothpick.

Heat oil in fryer. Fry apple burritos one at a time until golden
brown, turning over once. Drain on paper towels and sprinkle
with powdered sugar.

Fried Oreos

Makes over 50 cookies

1 large bag Oreo cookies
2 cups pancake mix
1-1/2 cups of milk
2 eggs
4 teaspoons oil

In a medium bowl, combine pancake mix, milk, eggs and oil until smooth. Dip Oreos into batter, make sure both sides are well covered. Put Oreos one at a time into the fryer, cooking till golden brown, turning once. Drain on paper towels and serve at once.

Fried Beaver Tails

Makes 4 dozen

1/2 cup warm water
5 teaspoons dry yeast
1 teaspoon sugar
1 cup warm milk
1/3 cup sugar
1-1/2 teaspoons salt
1 teaspoon vanilla
2 eggs
1/3 cup oil
4-1/4 to 5 cups unbleached all-purpose flour
Granulated sugar

In a large mixing bowl, stir together the yeast, warm water and teaspoon of sugar. Allow to stand a couple of minutes to allow yeast to proof.

Stir in remaining sugar, milk, vanilla, eggs, oil, salt and almost all of the flour to make a soft dough. On a floured surface, knead dough for five minutes, adding flour as needed to form a smooth, elastic dough.

Place in a greased bowl and cover with a clean tea towel. Let rise about 30-40 minutes. Gently punch down dough.

Pinch off a golf ball sized piece of dough. Roll out into an oval (this is going to be the beaver tail) and let rest, covered with a tea towel, while you are preparing the remaining dough into ovals.

Heat oil in fryer. Take the dough ovals and stretch them into a beaver tail just before cooking in hot oil. Add one beaver tail at a time to the hot oil, frying till golden, turning once.
Lift beaver tails out with tongs and drain on paper towels.
Sprinkle with sugar and serve.

Old Fashioned Crullers

Serves 4

1 yolk of egg, beaten
1 white of egg, beaten till peaked
1/4 cup of granulated sugar
1/4 teaspoon salt
1 tablespoonful of melted butter or margarine
1 cup flour
powdered sugar

In a small bowl, beat the sugar into the yolk. Then beat in the butter, fold in the white and add the flour and the salt. The dough must be firm enough to roll into a sheet about 1/3-inch thick, so add more flour if necessary.

Heat oil in the fryer. Cut dough into rectangular pieces (two by three inches), make four parallel slits in each equally distant from each other and the edges of the dough on all sides. Carefully lift up the second and fourth strips, to meet in the center, and cook in hot fat to a golden brown. Drain on paper towels and sprinkle with powdered sugar.

New Orleans Calas

Serves 4

2 cups cooked rice
3 eggs, beaten
1/2 cup sugar
1 teaspoon cinnamon
1 teaspoon nutmeg
1/2 teaspoon vanilla extract
2-1/4 teaspoons baking powder
3/4 to 1 cup flour
powdered sugar for garnish

In a large bowl, combine rice, eggs, sugar, cinnamon, nutmeg, vanilla and baking powder. Add just enough flour to hold the batter together (start with smaller measure and add as necessary).

Heat oil in the fryer. Drop batter by teaspoonfuls into hot oil. Fry in batches , but avoid over crowding. Cook till golden brown, about 7 minutes. Drain on paper towels and sprinkle with powdered sugar.

Banana Fritters

Serves 8

1-1/2 cups flour
2 teaspoons baking powder
2 tablespoons powdered sugar
1/4 teaspoon salt
2/3 cup milk
2 bananas, mashed
lemon juice
powdered sugar

In a large bowl, mix all dry ingredients and make a well in the center. In a smaller bowl, combine milk and egg, mixing well and add to dry ingredients. Fold in the mashed bananas. If it's too thick add milk, if it's too thin add flour. Batter should have the consistency of muffin batter.

Heat oil in fryer. Drop by the spoonfuls into the oil and cook till golden brown, turning once, about 5 minutes. Drain on paper towels. Sprinkle with powdered sugar and serve.

Fruity Fritters
Makes 24

1 cup sifted flour
1 teaspoon baking powder
1 tablespoon sugar
1/2 teaspoon salt
2 eggs, separated
1/2 cup milk
1 tablespoon oil
banana chunks, peaches, apples or fresh berries

In a small bowl, beat egg whites until stiff. Set aside. In a large bowl, sift together flour, baking powder, sugar and salt, making a well in the middle after well mixed. In a small bowl, beat egg yolks, milk, and oil into dry ingredients until well mixed. Fold beaten egg whites carefully into the batter.

Heat oil in fryer. Put banana chunks or other fruit in batter and fry for 3 to 4 minutes. Drain on paper towels and serve with powdered sugar sprinkled on the top.

Deep Fried Watermelon

1 watermelon, about 10 pounds
1/4 cup cornstarch
1-1/2 cups flour
2 eggs whites, beaten till soft peaks
2 to 4 tablespoons water
powdered sugar

Cut the watermelon in half and scoop out the flesh. Remove
any seeds from the flesh and cut the flesh into diamond shapes,
set aside. In a small bowl, mix the beaten egg whites with
cornstarch and water (start small) into a batter, the consistency
of muffin batter. In a shallow bowl, place the flour.

Heat the oil in the fryer. Dip the watermelon pieces in the
flour, then the batter and add to the fryer. Fry one at a time
until golden brown, turning once. Drain on paper towels and
serve. Sprinkle with powdered sugar if desired.

Fried Peaches with Raspberry Sauce
Serves 4

1 package (10 ounces) frozen sweetened raspberries, thawed
1 tablespoon Grand Marnier
2 (16 oz.) cans peach halves, drained
3 cups corn flake cereal, finely crushed
1 tablespoon flour
1 teaspoon ground cinnamon
1 egg

In a blender, combine raspberries and liqueur and blend until smooth. Set sauce aside.

Place peach halves on paper towels to drain. In a shallow dish, combine crushed cereal, flour and cinnamon. In a shallow bowl, place beaten egg. Dip each peach half in egg, then in the cereal crumb mixture, pressing to coat thoroughly.

Heat oil in the fryer. Fry a few peaches at a time, about 1 minute, or until golden brown, turning over once. Drain on paper towels. Serve warm in a bowl with sauce.

Champion Press, Ltd.

Visit our Cookbook Corner
or tips, ideas, recipes and more!

www.championpress.com